Make Financial Strong

Make Financial Strong

Easy to Understand how do you manage your money, expenses, debt, and achieving goals.

Subhajit Ghara

About The Author

Subhajit Ghara, holds a **Bachelor of Science (BSc)** degree and a **Post Graduate Diploma in Banking Service (PGDBS)**, bringing over **six years of hands-on experience in investing and financial management**. Passionate about simplifying complex financial concepts, he has dedicated their career to helping individuals make smarter money decisions.

In this book, they break down the essentials of **building financial strength** in **easy-to-understand language**, empowering readers to **invest wisely, grow wealth, and achieve financial freedom** — without the jargon.

This book is dedicated to my parents
Ranjan Ghara
and
Purnima Bera Ghara

I am grateful to God for blessing me with such
a loving and caring family.

Preface

The aim of this book is to guide you through the basics of money management and introduce you to concepts that will help you grow your wealth over time. From understanding budgeting and saving, to learning how to invest and plan for retirement, we will explore the essential tools you need to become financially strong.

My goal is not just to give you information, but to help you take action in your own life. You don't need to be a financial expert to make better money decisions; you just need the right knowledge and a willingness to start.

Whether you're looking to save for a goal, get out of debt, or start investing, this book will give you the confidence and the tools you need to take charge of your financial journey.

Kolkata
January, 2025   Subhajit Ghara

Acknowledgements

I would like to express my deepest gratitude to all those who contributed to the creation of this book. First and foremost, to my family, whose unwavering support and encouragement allowed me the time and space to write. Their belief in me has been a constant source of motivation.

A special thank you to my mentors and financial experts who generously shared their knowledge, insights, and experience. Without their guidance, much of the content in this book would not have been possible. Your expertise has shaped this work in ways words can hardly capture.

Lastly, to my readers: thank you for trusting this book as a resource in your journey to financially strong and security. May it help you navigate the world of mutual fund investing with confidence and clarity.

With sincere appreciation,
Subhajit Ghara

Contents

The basic of personal finance

Personal finance refers to the management of an individual's financial activities, including budgeting, saving, investing, managing debt, and planning for future financial needs. It involves understanding how to earn, spend, save, and invest money in ways that align with one's financial goals and security. Personal finance covers various aspects like creating a budget to control expenses, setting aside money for emergencies, investing for long-term goals like retirement, and ensuring financial protection through insurance and estate planning. It also involves making informed decisions about borrowing and managing debt wisely to avoid financial stress. Ultimately, personal finance is about making smart choices with money to achieve financial independence, stability, and peace of mind.

Let's start with a small story. Once upon a time in a small village in India, there lived a young girl named Rani. She lived with her grandfather, who was known in the village for his wisdom and hard work. Rani had just started earning her own money by helping at the local shop after school. Excited with her first income, she bought clothes, sweets, and even a new phone, all in the span of a few weeks. She thought that she would always have money coming her way and that there was no need to save.

One day, Rani's grandfather, seeing how she spent her earnings so quickly, decided to teach her a valuable lesson.

He took her to the village market. There, they saw a poor farmer who had just finished selling his vegetables. He was counting the little money he earned and putting it into a small, tattered cloth pouch. The farmer smiled and said, "I don't make a lot, but I save a little every day, no matter how small the amount. That way, even when times are tough, I have something to rely on."

Rani was curious and asked her grandfather, "Why does the farmer save so much? Doesn't he have enough to live on?"

Her grandfather replied, "Let me show you something, Rani."

He took her to a nearby temple, where an elderly priest was making offerings of rice to the gods. "This rice," the grandfather said, "was saved by the farmer each day. Small amounts, but over time, they add up. Just like money. When we don't manage our resources carefully, we may run out when we need them most."

Rani didn't understand fully, so her grandfather gave her a simple task. He asked her to save a part of her earnings every month, even if it was just a little bit. He also told her to be mindful of her spending, and not to let her desires for things that weren't necessary take control of her decisions.

Months passed, and Rani began to save a small portion of her earnings, just like the farmer. She still spent money on things she enjoyed but became more thoughtful about it. When an unexpected family wedding came up, Rani was able to contribute without worrying about running out of money. She was also able to buy a new set of books for her studies without asking her family for extra money.

One day, a storm hit the village, and the crops were destroyed. Many villagers struggled, but Rani noticed that the farmer, who had saved diligently, was able to provide food for his family through the difficult times. He even helped others who were in need.

Rani learned that saving money wasn't about being rich; it was about being wise and secure. With the money she saved, she had the peace of mind to face challenges that came her way. She also realized that money could bring freedom — not just to buy things, but to have the strength to deal with life's uncertainties.

The Importance of Financial Literacy

In today's fast-paced world, managing personal finances is more important than ever. Financial literacy is the knowledge and understanding of how money works, which enables individuals to make informed and effective decisions about their financial resources. It includes everything from budgeting, saving, and investing, to managing debt and preparing for future financial needs. Unfortunately, many people lack financial knowledge, which can lead to poor financial decisions and unnecessary stress. With the right financial education, individuals can unlock opportunities, build wealth, and gain control over their financial futures.

In this chapter, we will explore the critical aspects of financial literacy and how it shapes a person's life. Understanding the importance of financial literacy can help individuals avoid common pitfalls, seize financial opportunities, and create a secure financial future for themselves and their families.

***

Setting Financial Goals

Setting financial goals is the process of identifying specific, measurable objectives related to your money that you want to achieve within a given timeframe. It helps you prioritize your spending, saving, and investing decisions, providing a clear roadmap for your financial future. Financial goals can range from short-term objectives like buying a new phone to long-term ambitions such as saving for retirement or purchasing a home. By setting goals, you are creating a vision for your financial well-being and directing your efforts toward achieving it.

Types of Financial Goals

1. *Short-Term Goals:* These goals typically have a timeframe of up to one year. They are usually small, achievable targets that

help build a strong financial foundation. Examples include saving for a vacation, buying a new gadget, or paying off a credit card balance. Short-term goals provide quick wins, which help build financial discipline and momentum.

2.*Medium-Term Goals:* Medium-term goals typically span between one to five years. These goals may require more planning and saving but are still within reach. Examples include buying a car, funding a child's education, or building an emergency savings fund. Medium-term goals often require consistent saving and budgeting to reach.

3.*Long-Term Goals:* Long-term financial goals typically take five years or more to accomplish and require extensive planning and consistent effort. Examples include purchasing a home, saving for retirement, or starting a business. Achieving these goals often requires larger investments, discipline, and long-term financial planning.

Importance of Settings Financial Goals

Setting financial goals is important because it gives you direction and purpose in managing your money. Without clear goals, it's easy to get sidetracked and make impulsive financial decisions that can hinder your progress. Financial goals act as a guide to help you prioritize how you spend, save, and invest. They help you focus on what truly matters and avoid unnecessary expenses.

Moreover, financial goals serve as a motivating factor. Knowing that you are working towards something important, such as a secure retirement or a home, gives you the drive to make sacrifices in the present, like cutting back on spending or increasing your savings rate. Achieving financial goals, even small ones, can provide a sense of accomplishment and boost your confidence in managing money.

Additionally, having clear financial goals helps you create a budget and allocate resources effectively. It forces you to plan for the future, whether that's putting aside money for an emergency fund or investing for long-term growth. This proactive approach not only increases your financial security but also reduces stress, as you will be prepared for both expected and unexpected financial events.

Guide to achieving your Financial Goals

The SMART framework is an effective method for setting and achieving financial goals. SMART stands for Specific, Measurable, Achievable, Relevant, and Time-bound. By using this structure, you can create clear, actionable goals that will increase your chances of success.

- *Specific*

  A specific goal is clear and focused. It answers the questions: What do I want to accomplish? Why is this goal important? Who is involved? Where will it take place? A vague goal like "I want to save more money" won't help you take action. Instead, a specific goal might be, "I want to save ₹2,000 for an emergency fund." This gives you a clear target to work towards.

Example: "I want to save ₹2,000 in the next 6 months to create an emergency fund."

- *Measurable*

  A measurable goal means that you can track your progress and determine when you've achieved it. This step involves deciding how you'll measure success and whether you'll need a tool like a budget, app, or spreadsheet to track your progress. Setting measurable goals helps you stay on track and adjust your efforts if needed.

Example: "I will save ₹400 every month for the next 5 months to reach my ₹2,000 emergency fund goal."

- *Achievable*

  An achievable goal is realistic and attainable, considering your current financial situation, resources, and time. Setting an unrealistic goal, such as saving ₹30,000 in two months when your income is limited, may leave you feeling overwhelmed and discouraged. It's important to challenge yourself, but make sure the goal is possible given your circumstances.

Example: "I will adjust my budget to save ₹500 a month by cutting back on non-essential expenses, such as dining out or subscription services."

- ***Relevant***

   A relevant goal is one that aligns with your broader financial plans and life priorities. It should be meaningful and have a significant impact on your long-term financial well-being. Before setting a financial goal, ask yourself how it fits into your bigger picture. It's essential to ensure that your financial goals matter to you and are aligned with your values.

Example: "Building an emergency fund is relevant to my financial security because it will help me handle unexpected expenses without going into debt."

- ***Time-bound***

   A time-bound goal has a clear deadline or timeframe for completion. This provides urgency and helps keep you accountable. Without a timeline, it's easy to procrastinate or lose sight of the goal. Setting a deadline encourages consistent action and allows you to track your progress against a set schedule.

Example: "I will save ₹10,000 for an emergency fund by the end of December, ensuring I have a financial cushion for the new year."

***

Budgeting and Expense Management

A **budget** is a financial plan that helps you manage your income and expenses, allowing you to control how your money is allocated each month. It is a tool that outlines where your money comes from (income) and how it will be spent (expenses), ensuring you live within your means and can achieve financial goals like saving, investing, and reducing debt.

Expenses are the costs you incur while maintaining your lifestyle, which can be categorized into fixed and variable types, such as rent, groceries, utilities, entertainment, and debt payments. Budgets and expenses matter because they provide a clear picture of your financial situation, preventing overspending, helping you save, and allowing for better decision-making about your money.

Why Budgeting Matters

Budgeting is essential for financial stability and achieving long-term goals.
  i.   Helps You Achieve Financial Goals.
  ii.   Avoids and Eliminates Debt.
  iii. Builds Financial Security.
  iv.   Improves Money Management Skills.
  v.   Prevents Overspending.

50-30-20 budget rule

- **Needs (50%)** – Essential Expenses

Half of your income should cover necessities—things you must pay for to live: e.g., rent, utilities, groceries, transportation, insurance etc.

- **Wants (30%)** – Lifestyle Choices

This portion is for **non-essential** spending that improves your quality of life: e.g., shopping (clothes, electronics), travel, entertainment, dining out etc.

- **Savings & Debt Repayment (20%)** – Financial Future
  This helps you build wealth and financial security: emergency fund, investment, retirement savings etc.

Tools for budgeting:

Budgeting tools help you track income, expenses, and financial goals efficiently. Some of the best tools are for effective budgeting: Budgeting Method (50-30-20 rule), Spreadsheets, Financial Planners & Journals, Banking app, Credit card statements etc.

***

Saving Strategies

Saving strategies are techniques and approaches used to set aside money for future use, whether for emergencies, big purchases, or long-term goals like retirement. The main goal of saving is to accumulate funds that will be used to meet financial needs or desires without relying on credit or loans. Effective saving strategies can help individuals build wealth, achieve financial security, and prepare for unexpected expenses. The key to successful saving lies in discipline, planning, and the use of appropriate saving methods that align with one's financial goals.

Building an Emergency Fund

An **emergency fund** is money set aside to cover unexpected expenses like medical bills, car repairs, or job loss. It acts as a safety net, preventing you from relying on credit cards or loans when life throws surprise your way. Having an emergency fund gives you peace of mind and financial security.

Building an emergency fund is simple. Start by setting a small goal, like saving ₹5,000 to ₹10,000. Then, slowly work towards saving **three to six months'** worth of living expenses. Put this money in a separate savings account. To save consistently, set up automatic transfers, cut back on non-essential spending (like eating out or subscriptions), and use any extra income to grow your fund. Over time, even small savings will add up, giving you financial stability when unexpected costs arise.

Automating savings

It means setting up your bank account to transfer money into your savings automatically. This helps you save without thinking about it and ensures that you always set aside money before spending on other things. It's one of the easiest ways to build good financial habits and reach your goals faster.

For example, if you earn ₹30,000 per month, you can set up an automatic transfer of ₹3,000 (10%) to a savings account as soon as your salary is credited. This way, you save consistently without worrying about it.

Over time, this small step will help you build an emergency fund, plan for future expenses, and achieve financial security effortlessly.

High-Yield Savings Accounts

A high-yield savings account offers a higher interest rate than a regular savings account, allowing your savings to grow faster. These accounts are usually offered by online banks and are a great option for building an emergency fund.

Certificates of Deposit (CDs)

CDs are time-based deposit accounts where you commit to keeping your money in the account for a fixed term, ranging from a few months to several years. In return, you earn a fixed interest rate that is higher than a regular savings account.

The downside is that you cannot access the money before the maturity date without paying a penalty.

Auto-Sweep FD

An Auto-Sweep Fixed Deposit (FD) is a smart way to save for emergencies while earning higher interest. It combines the benefits of a savings account and an FD, ensuring that your money is both accessible and growing at a better rate.

Money Market Accounts

A money market account offers higher interest rates than a typical savings account. These accounts are a good balance between safety and earning potential, making them a great option for those looking to save while still keeping their money easily accessible.

***

Debt Management

Debt management refers to the process of managing and repaying outstanding debts in a systematic and strategic way. It involves understanding the types of debt you owe, prioritizing repayment, and developing a plan to reduce or eliminate the debt over time.

Effective debt management is crucial for improving financial health, reducing financial stress, and achieving long-term financial goals. It requires discipline, careful planning, and often a change in spending habits to regain control over one's finances.

Types of Debt

Secured Debt:

This type of debt is backed by collateral, meaning if the borrower defaults, the lender can claim the asset. Common examples include mortgages and car loans. Secured debt typically has lower interest rates because the lender has collateral as security.

Unsecured Debt:

This debt is not backed by collateral and includes credit card balances, personal loans, medical bills, and student loans. Unsecured debt tends to have higher interest rates because the lender assumes greater risk.

Revolving Debt:

Revolving debt allows you to borrow up to a set limit, pay it down, and borrow again. Credit cards are the most common example of revolving debt. As long as you make minimum payments, you can continue borrowing, but high-interest rates can lead to growing balances if not managed properly.

Instalment Debt:

Instalment debt involves borrowing a fixed amount of money to be repaid in equal instalment over time. Examples include mortgages, auto loans, and student loans. These debts have a set repayment schedule, which helps with planning and budgeting.

<u>Methods of Debt Repayment:</u>

Snowball Method:

This method involves paying off your smallest debt first while making minimum payments on larger debts. Once the smallest debt is paid off, the freed-up money is then applied to the next smallest debt, and so on. This method is popular because it provides quick wins and boosts motivation as you see debts disappearing.

Avalanche Method:

The debt avalanche method focuses on paying off high-interest debt first, regardless of the amount owed. After paying off the highest-interest debt, you move on to the next highest-interest debt, and so on. This method saves the most money in interest over time but may feel slower at first if larger debts are low-interest.

Consolidation:

Debt consolidation involves combining multiple debts into one loan with a lower interest rate. This can simplify repayments and reduce the total interest paid over time. Options for consolidation include personal loans or transferring credit card balances to a lower-interest card.

Balance Transfer:

With a balance transfer, you move high-interest credit card debt to a new credit card offering a 0% introductory interest rate. This gives you a break from paying high interest, but it's important to pay off the balance before the introductory period ends to avoid steep interest rates.

***

Investing for the Future

Investing for the future is the process of allocating money towards assets or opportunities that are expected to grow in value over time, with the goal of achieving financial stability and wealth accumulation.

Unlike saving, which typically involves putting money in a low-interest account, investing aims to generate returns through various financial instruments, such as stocks, bonds, real estate, or mutual funds. The primary objective is to ensure that your money works for you, helping you achieve long-term goals like purchasing a home, funding education, or retiring comfortably.

Understanding Investment

Investments can range from low-risk options like government bonds to higher-risk investments like stocks or startups. Each investment type has its own characteristics, such as how it generates returns (e.g., dividends, interest, capital gains) and the level of risk associated with it. It's potential for growth, income, and its associated risks is essential for building a diversified and successful investment portfolio.

Risk and Return are fundamental concepts in investing.

Risk refers to the possibility that an investment's value might decrease, while return is the profit or gain made from an investment.

Generally, investments with higher potential returns come with higher risks, and those with lower risks offer more stable but lower returns.

For example, stocks offer the potential for high returns, but they can also be volatile and lose value, while bonds are more stable but typically provide lower returns. Balancing risk and return are a personal decision and should align with an individual's financial goals, timeline, and risk tolerance.

Retirement Accounts

In India, retirement accounts help people save money for their post-work life. These accounts offer tax benefits, steady income after retirement, and financial security. Some common types and their benefits:

Public Provident Fund (PPF)

- PPF falls under the EEE (Exempt-Exempt-Exempt) category.
- Investment, interest earned, and maturity amount are all tax-free under Section 80C of the Income Tax Act.
- PPF is government-backed, making it a risk-free investment.
- The interest rate is revised quarterly by the government, usually around 7-8% per annum.
- The minimum lock-in period is 15 years, ensuring long-term growth.
- You can extend it in blocks of 5 years after maturity.

- Minimum deposit: ₹500 per year and Maximum deposit: ₹1.5 lakh per year.
- Unlike stocks or mutual funds, PPF is not linked to the stock market, making it a stable investment.

Employees' Provident Fund (EPF)

The Employees' Provident Fund (EPF) is a retirement savings scheme for salaried employees in India, managed by the Employees' Provident Fund Organisation (EPFO). Both the employee and employer contribute a portion of the salary every month, helping build a retirement corpus.

- The amount grows with monthly contributions + interest and can be withdrawn at retirement.
- EPF is under the EEE (Exempt-Exempt-Exempt) category, meaning: Contributions are tax-deductible under Section 80C. Interest earned is tax-free (if withdrawn after 5 years). The final withdrawal amount is tax-free.
- Employee contributes 12% of Basic Salary + DA.

- Employer also contributes 12%, but a part of it goes towards Employee Pension Scheme (EPS).
- EPF offers a government-backed interest rate (usually 8-8.5% per annum).
- Returns are risk-free and not linked to the stock market.
- Employees become eligible for a monthly pension after 58 years of age if they have contributed for at least 10 years.

National Pension System (NPS)

The National Pension System (NPS) is a government-backed retirement savings scheme open to all Indian citizens. It helps individuals build a pension corpus for financial security after retirement. NPS invests in a mix of equity (stocks) and debt (bonds), ensuring good returns over time.

- Under Section 80CCD (1): Up to ₹1.5 lakh per year is tax-deductible.
- Additional ₹50,000 deduction under Section 80CCD(1B).
- Employer contributions (up to 10% of salary) are tax-free under Section 80CCD (2).

- NPS invests in a mix of equities, corporate bonds, and government securities.
- Choose between Auto mode (automatic asset allocation) or Active mode (self-managed).
- Option to invest in Equity (E), Corporate Bonds (C), and Government Securities (G).
- Easy online account management through PRAN (Permanent Retirement Account Number).

Senior Citizens Savings Scheme (SCSS)

The Senior Citizens Savings Scheme (SCSS) is a government-backed savings scheme designed for senior citizens (60+ years) in India. It offers guaranteed returns, regular income, and tax benefits, making it a safe and reliable investment option for retirees.

- SCSS offers a **higher interest rate** compared to fixed deposits (FDs) and savings accounts.
- The interest rate is revised every quarter and is usually **around 7-8% per annum**.

- SCSS is backed by the **Government of India**, making it a **risk-free** investment.
- Deposits of up to **₹1.5 lakh per year** are eligible for a **tax deduction** under **Section 80C**.
- However, interest earned **is taxable** if it exceeds ₹50,000 per year.
- SCSS has a **5-year tenure**, which can be extended by **3 more years** after maturity.

***

Financial Planning for life stages

Financial planning is the process of managing money wisely at different stages of life. As you grow, your financial goals and needs change.

Starting Out (Early Career: 20s-30s)

This is when you start earning money and building a financial foundation.

- Create a Budget – Track income and expenses to save money.
- Emergency Fund – Save at least 3-6 months' expenses in a bank account.
- Avoid Debt – Clear credit card bills and student loans.
- Invest Early – Start investing in mutual funds, stocks, or PPF to grow wealth.

- Buy Health & Term Insurance – Protect yourself and your family.

Family Planning Stage (Mid-Career: 30s-40s)

This is when people **get married, have kids, or buy a house**.
- Buy a Home – Take a home loan within your budget.
- Save for Kids' Education – Invest in PPF, Sukanya Samriddhi, or mutual funds.
- Increase Emergency Fund – Cover 6-12 months' expenses in case of job loss.
- Plan for Retirement – Invest in NPS, EPF, or SIPs for long-term wealth.
- Get Life Insurance – Buy a term plan to secure your family.

Pre-Retirement (Late Career: 40s-50s)

This is when you **prepare for retirement and reduce financial risks**.
- Clear Loans & Debt – Pay off home loans and other debts before retirement.

- Boost Retirement Savings – Increase investment in PPF, NPS, or retirement funds.
- Medical & Health Cover – Get a comprehensive health insurance policy.
- Diversify Investments – Reduce risky investments and shift to safer options like FDs, bonds, or SCSS.

Retirement Stage (60+ years)

Now, you **stop working and rely on savings & pensions**.

- Secure Monthly Income – Invest in Senior Citizens Savings Scheme (SCSS), Post Office Monthly Income Scheme (POMIS), or annuities.
- Manage Expenses – Avoid unnecessary spending and focus on needs.
- Health & Emergency Funds – Keep money aside for medical expenses.
- Safe & Low-Risk Investments – Avoid stock market risks; choose fixed deposits or bonds.
- Enjoy Life – Travel, pursue hobbies, and spend time with family stress-free.

Avoid Common financial Pitfalls

Many people make money mistakes that can lead to stress, debt, and financial insecurity. Avoiding these common financial pitfalls can help you achieve long-term stability and wealth.

Overspending

Spending more than you earn, leading to debt and financial struggles, using credit cards irresponsibly or taking loans for unnecessary expenses.

How to Avoid It:

- Use cash or UPI instead of credit cards for everyday purchases.

- Track spending with budgeting apps like Walnut, Money Manager, or Google Sheets.
- Create a budget using the 50-30-20 rule (50% Needs, 30% Wants, 20% Savings).
- Differentiate between wants and needs — buy what you need, not what you "feel like" buying.

Ignoring Retirement Savings

Many people delay saving for retirement because they think they have plenty of time. If you start later, then it is harder to build a big retirement fund. Without savings, you may struggle financially after retirement.

How to Avoid It:

- Start investing early — even small amounts grow big due to compounding.
- Invest in PPF, EPF, NPS, and mutual funds (SIP).
- If salaried, maximize EPF contributions for long-term benefits.
- Use an NPS calculator to estimate how much you'll need at retirement.

Lack of an Emergency Fund

Not having backup money for job loss, medical issues, or unexpected expenses. Facing stress and financial instability due to lack of savings. So, saving is must important.
How to Avoid It:

- Save at least 3-6 months' worth of living expenses in a separate bank account or FD.
- If you're self-employed, save 6-12 months' expenses.
- Keep it liquid—don't invest emergency funds in risky assets like stocks.
- Automate savings—set up a recurring deposit to grow the fund gradually.

***

Creating a Financial Legacy

A financial legacy means leaving behind wealth, assets, and financial security for your family and future generations. It's about building wealth wisely and ensuring your loved ones benefit even after you're gone. To create a strong legacy, start by saving and investing early in secure options like mutual funds, real estate, and retirement plans. Protect your wealth by getting life insurance and creating a will to ensure smooth inheritance. Teach your children smart money habits so they can continue managing wealth responsibly. A financial legacy isn't just about money—it's about providing security, opportunities, and a better future for your family.

<u>Estate Planning</u>

Estate planning is the process of deciding how your money, property, and assets will be managed or passed on to your family after you're gone. It ensures that your loved ones receive what you intend for them without legal troubles. The most important step is writing a will, which clearly states who will inherit your wealth. You can also set up nominees for bank accounts, insurance, and investments to make things easier. If you have a large estate, consider a trust to manage assets wisely. Good estate planning helps avoid family disputes, reduce taxes, and secure your family's future.

<u>Teaching financial literacy</u>

Start by teaching how to create a budget to track income and expenses, and how to set aside money for future needs, like an emergency fund. Help them understand the importance of saving for retirement and how investments like stocks, mutual funds, or PPF can grow wealth over time. Finally, teach about setting financial goals and planning for the future, so they can be financially secure and independent.

Financial literacy is not just about numbers—it's about making smart choices with money for a better, stress-free life.

<u>Philanthropy</u>

Philanthropy is the act of donating money, time, or resources to help improve the well-being of others and make a positive impact on society. It's about using personal wealth or influence to support causes like education, healthcare, poverty alleviation, environmental protection, and more.

Philanthropy can take many forms:
- Monetary donations to charity or non-profits.
- Volunteering time to help others or contribute skills to community projects.
- Building foundations or creating programs that support long-term change.

It's not just about giving large sums of money—every small contribution, whether it's money, time, or effort, can help make a difference. Through philanthropy, individuals and organizations aim to create a better world and leave a positive legacy for future generations.

***

The Power of Compounding

The power of compounding is one of the most important principles in investing. It means that when you earn interest or returns on your investments, not only do you earn on your original amount (called the principal), but you also earn interest on the interest you've already accumulated. Over time, this leads to your money growing much faster than if you were just earning interest on the initial amount.

A Story of Ram, Rahul, and Sunil

Once upon a time, three friends—Ram, Rahul, and Sunil—were all in their early 20s, just starting their careers. They had different approaches to managing their money, and their decisions would have a big impact on their financial future.

Ram: The Early Investor

Ram believed in starting early. As soon as he began working, he decided to invest ₹5,000 every month in a mutual fund. He chose a high-growth equity mutual fund with an average annual return of 12%.

Monthly Investment: ₹5,000

Annual Return: 12%

Investment Period: 30 years (until he turned 55)

By the time Ram reached 55 years old, his small, regular investments had grown significantly due to compounding. Even though he only invested ₹5,000 each month, the value of his investments was ₹1.7 crore.

This shows how starting early, even with a small amount, can result in huge returns due to the power of compounding.

Rahul: The Late Starter

Rahul was a bit more focused on enjoying his life. He did not think about saving or investing until he was in his 40s. At 40, he realized the importance of saving for the future, so he decided to start investing the same amount as Ram—₹5,000 per month—but only from age 40 to 55.

> Monthly Investment: ₹5,000
> Annual Return: 12%
> Investment Period: 15 years (from age 40 to 55)

By the time Rahul reached 55, his total investment amounted to only ₹29.4 lakh. While this is a good amount, it is far less than what Ram had accumulated, because Rahul missed out on 15 years of compounding growth.

Sunil: The non-investor

Sunil, on the other hand, didn't believe in investing at all. He preferred to keep his money in a savings account earning only around 4% interest. He saved ₹5,000 every month but kept it in the bank.

> Monthly Savings: ₹5,000

Interest Rate: 4%

Investment Period: 30 years (until he turned 55)

By the time Sunil turned 55, his total savings in the bank was just ₹31.6 lakh. While it's good that he saved regularly, his money didn't grow much due to the low interest rate. His savings didn't benefit from the growth potential that investments offer.

The story of Ram, Rahul, and Sunil teaches us a valuable lesson: Starting early with investments can lead to much bigger wealth over time.

***

Notes:

Books By this Authors: